MIGHTY MILITARY MACHINES

Humvees

A 4D BOOK

by Matt Scheff

PEBBLE
a capstone imprint

Little Pebble is published by Pebble
1710 Roe Crest Drive, North Mankato,
Minnesota 56003
www.mycapstone.com

Library of Congress Cataloging-in-Publication Data
Library of Congress Cataloging-in-Publication data is available from the Library of Congress website.

ISBN 978-1-9771-0109-9 (hardcover)
ISBN 978-1-9771-0115-0 (paperback)
ISBN 978-1-9771-0121-1 (eBook PDF)

Editorial Credits
Marissa Kirkman, editor; Heidi Thompson, designer;
Jo Miller, media researcher; Tori Abraham, production specialist

Photo Credits
iStockphoto: Rockfinder, 5; U.S. Air Force photo by Airman 1st Class Kaleb Snay, 17, Staff Sgt.
Matthew Smith, 11; U.S. Air National Guard photo by Master Sgt. Matt Hecht, 9; U.S. Army National
Guard photo by Sgt. Adrian Borunda, 19, Staff Sgt. Brian A. Barbour, 21; U.S. Army photo by Spc
John Russell, cover, Visual Information Specialist Paolo Bovo, 13; U.S. Marine Corps Combat Camera
photo by Lance Cpl. Eryn L. Edelman, 15, U.S. Marine Corps photo by Lance Cpl. Amy Phan, 7
Design Elements: Shutterstock: Zerbor

This is a Capstone 4D book!

Want fun videos that go with this book?

Just visit www.capstone4d.com

Use this password
humvees.01099

Table of Contents

What is a Humvee?

Zoom!

A truck speeds over the land.

It is a Humvee.

Humvees in Action

Humvees are army trucks.

They hold cargo.

Humvees carry soldiers.
The trucks bring them
where they need to go.

TIE-DOWN

This Humvee helps people.
It takes them to safety.

Look up!

This Humvee drops

from a plane!

Humvee Parts

Humvees have big tires.

The tires have deep tread.

They roll over the land.

TIE-DOWN

tread

Roar! This truck has

a strong engine.

It powers the truck.

Bang! Boom!

Humvees have big guns.

They have missiles too.

Humvees are strong.

They keep soldiers safe.

They help them do their jobs.

Glossary

army—a group of soldiers trained to fight on land

cargo—objects carried by a ship, aircraft, or other vehicle

engine—a machine that makes the power needed to move something

missile—an explosive weapon that is thrown or shot at a distant target

soldier—a person who is in the military

tread—the bumps and grooves on a vehicle's tire that help the tire grip the land or road

Read More

Doeden, Matt. *The U.S. Army.* The U.S. Military Branches. North Mankato, Minn.: Capstone Press, 2018.

Graubart, Norman D. *Armored Trucks.* Giants on the Road. New York: PowerKids Press, 2015.

Willis, John. *Humvees.* Mighty Military Machines. New York: AV2 by Weigl, 2017.

Internet Sites

Use FactHound to find Internet sites related to this book.

Visit *www.facthound.com*
Just type in 9781977101099 and go.

Check out projects, games and lots more at
www.capstonekids.com

Critical Thinking Questions

1. Which part gives a Humvee its power?

2. What do soldiers use Humvees for?

3. How does the deep tread on the tires help the Humvee?

Index